LOVE NOTEZ

From My Heart To Yours:

AN OPEN JOURNAL FILLED WITH NOTES OF LOVE, JOY, PEACE, & ENCOURAGEMENT!

RACQUEL PECULIAR COONEY

iUniverse®

LOVE NOTEZ
FROM MY HEART TO YOURS: AN OPEN JOURNAL FILLED
WITH NOTES OF LOVE, JOY, PEACE, & ENCOURAGEMENT!

iUniverse books may be ordered through booksellers or by contacting:

iUniverse
1663 Liberty Drive
Bloomington, IN 47403
www.iuniverse.com
844-349-9409

Because of the dynamic nature of the Internet, any web addresses or links contained in this book may have changed since publication and may no longer be valid. The views expressed in this work are solely those of the author and do not necessarily reflect the views of the publisher, and the publisher hereby disclaims any responsibility for them.

Any people depicted in stock imagery provided by Getty Images are models, and such images are being used for illustrative purposes only. Certain stock imagery © Getty Images.

ISBN: 978-1-6632-0482-0 (sc)
ISBN: 978-1-6632-0483-7 (e)

Library of Congress Control Number: 2020913184

Print information available on the last page.

iUniverse rev. date: 08/11/2020

DEDICATION

I dedicated this book to every purpose-filled individual who chooses to always thrive in the mist of adversity. May this book empower you, and give you the dose of GOD-FIDENCE and WHOLENESS that you need to persevere and become all that God has created you to be. May God continue to bless you and hold your heart in the palm of his hands.

Special Thank You:

To my lord and savior JESUS CHRIST thank you for loving me, and seeing me properly for it birthed the un-shattering God-centered momentum to walk in my purpose and remain Beyond Peculiar while doing so.

To my parents and my right hand man, Monique Cooney- Echols, Henry Black, and Manuel Echols (brother). Thank you for the cultivation, direction and constant push to obtain every dream. To the one who expanded my realm of being my son Jeremiah L. Criswell. Also known as my PURPOSE-Filled SEED. Thank you for giving mommy a new and expanded realm of identity and influence. Last but certainly not least my two G.G's. My guardian angel Grace B. Cooney, thank you for birthing the ropes of writing and story-telling within me and teaching me to always walk and create with style and grace. My Granny Glo, thank you for teaching me how to glow from the inside out. This love note here is for all of you. Here's to us reaching beyond the surface and producing GENERATIONAL WHOLENESS.

-Racquel Peculiar Cooney

INTRODUCTION

May the words from my heart be soothing to your soul. May each love note bring forth wholeness and ensure you that you're not alone. Allow my words to lock hands with your heart and break forth the reassurance to PUSH & for some simply to start. Words are power and they become the manifestation of our existence once spoken as well as written. This here is my ultimate love note to you; may God continue to guide you through.

/bēˈänd/ /pəˈkyō͞ olyər/
A movement that encourages individuals to be true to their AUTHENTIC selves. Whom God has created them to be!

JOURNAL #1

It's NEVER about being better than anyone it's ALL about knowing YOUR worth, LOVING YOURSELF & fulfilling YOUR PURPOSE!

JOURNAL #2

PERCEPTION Is REALITY ....What We Believe Is What We'll Receive!!!! TODAY, I want to encourage EVERYONE that stumbles across this Post THAT THERE'S A TREMENDOUS BLESSING THAT IS WAITING FOR YOU ON THE OTHER SIDE......However, In order for us to receive the Blessing (JOB, CAREER, OPPORTUNITY, SPOUSE, BUSINESS, BOOK, FINANCES ETC...) We have to be PREPARED For the Blessing.... Often times we PRAY for the blessing without PREPARING For the Blessing. PREPARATION IS KEY during the course of Divine Destiny!!! SO TODAY DURING YOUR ALONE TIME I WANT YOU TO ASK YOURSELF A SERIOUS QUESTION.... AM I TRULY READY FOR WHAT I AM PRAYING FOR? We have to PREPARE For What We Pray For....We spend a lot of time PRAYING when we need to spend JUST AS MUCH TIME PREPARING....Because without preparation we will lose the very thing we've prayed & asked God to give us. Because in all actuality if God were to bless us with what we desire right now at this very moment, we wouldn't even know how to handle the blessing because we lack PREPARATION!!!! IN ORDER TO RECEIVE YOU MUST PREPARE......

JOURNAL #3

GOD WILL USE US RIGHT WHERE WE ARE When We Feel UNQUALIFIED That's When HIS HAND Opens The Door(s) Of QUALIFICATION!

I CONTINUE To Smile Because God Is Doing So Much More Than What I (We) Can See Right Now!!!

JOURNAL #4

Mirror, mirror on the wall

Allow me to see What GOD sees

A reflection of My BEAUTY, FLAWS & ALL

Hello there beautiful, Yes YOU. I want to take the time out to acknowledge & awaken the AUTHENTIC beauty that lives on the inside of you.

I want you to know that you're a Gift....One of the most precious gifts here on this earth. YES, I Said It Now Allow that statement/TRUTH to saturate your mind for a moment......

You're a gift & this world needs your gifts. Never be ashamed of WHO YOU ARE (From the inside out) OR WHERE YOU HAVE BEEN.

In a world that is trying to diminish the true meaning of SELF LOVE & VALUE....It is my prayer that you NEVER forget who you are & WHO'S you are GOD Created YOU just the way you are SIMPLY, UNDENIABLY, AND PECULIARLY BEAUTIFUL!!!

SO Shine that Beyond Peculiar Light of Yours & EXHIBIT YOUR PERSONAL FORM OF BEAUTY & Watch how it awakens the beauty in others.

This one is for the "ewww she's too big" or the "omg I can see her bones she's so small" What they fail to realize Is WE ARE CHILDREN OF A KING THERE'S BEAUTY THAT EXUDES FROM US ALL.

JOURNAL #5

IMPERATIVE/INFLUENTIAL MESSAGE:

It's not about who did it first....it's about you doing what GOD has called you to do and Shinning YOUR Beyond Peculiar LIGHT While doing so.

I don't believe in "competition" I'm a firm believer that what God has for you is SIMPLY FOR YOU....& nothing nor anyone can take that from you!!!

JOURNAL #6

Most People Cringe At The Idea & Thought Of Discomfort.....BUT GOD I THANK YOU For Placing Me In The Realm Of Discomfort & Unfamiliarity It Allows Me To Have & Gain Unshakable Faith & Dependence In YOU & ONLY YOU!!!

"Get Comfortable Being Uncomfortable...Get Confident Being Uncertain... Don't Give Up Just Because Something Is Hard...PUSH THROUGH your challenges, It's What Makes You Grow"

As Sarah Jakes Roberts would say EMBRACE THEE UNCOMFORTABLE TO BECOME UNSTOPPABLE.

I Have Faith In YOU (Yes you reading this) & I Believe In You BUT More importantly, GOD Believes in you....Now GO Get What's YOURS!!!!

JOURNAL #7

JOURNAL SNIPPET: Being a young woman of self-love and value is a lot harder than it seems.... It's this bittersweet emotion that seems to never leave....It's knowing what's right but constantly being offered what's wrong....it's finding the "perfect guy" & months later being left all alone.... It's battling What's real Vs. What I want to feel....It's a constant prayer to God "Is Love really real?".

"Maybe It's True......

There is no man that will WAIT & Truly love you for you"

NO They're wrong You're worth more than a touch & a few moans......

Just Continue to be a light to EVERY man you encounter & as you pray for him...watch his love for God grow stronger!!!! It'll be because of your prayers that he can now see...The true beauty of Value & that the Cost isn't cheap!

I speak life and love over the men of my generation. I pray that they receive better exemplification of Men. Specifically Men of God and that they continue to enlighten them on how women should be treated

JOURNAL #8

JESUS LOVES ME......That Alone Does Something To Me On The Inside....I Never Have To Look For Love In Anyone Nor In Anything Or In All The Wrong Places Because HIS LOVE Is NEVER ENDING Nor Has It Ever Failed Me....I'll ALWAYS Rock With Him....WHY?! Well, He's The Only One That Loves Me In spite Of...No Matter How Many Times I've Failed Him His Love Never Failed Me....

·Oh & To All My Sisters Out There (Yea You Reading This) If You Don't Know Him Get To Know Him...He's Personally My Fave

And Check This, Jesus Will NEVER Wake Up & Decide He Wants To Leave. You Don't Believe Me?! Give Him A Try. Just Once He'll Blow Your Mind ....I'm in Love with Him & I Can't Get Enough of Him!

JOURNAL #9

"SOCIETY" (s), Definition Of "Beauty" Seriously Makes Me Want To Puke...It's So Fake & Unrealistic......& It TRULY Angers Me Because There Are So Many Men Who Over Look Natural Beauty Due To The Perpetuated Presence Of What I Like To Call "Fraudulent Beauty" .... They've Totally Forgotten What A NATURAL BLACK WOMAN Looks Like.....In This Day & Age So Many Feel That Beauty Is Defined By The Amount Of Makeup, Weave, & Materialistic Things That You Have/Wear, AND THAT'S A LIE....

That Expectation Has Caused So Many Young Women to Feel As If They're Not Beautiful....AND I CANT/WON'T ALLOW THAT TO HAPPEN!!!!

So TODAY I challenge each WOMAN that is currently reading this love note TO OWN YOUR NATURAL BEAUTY....Look in that mirror & TRULY LOVE/OWN What You See...Our Beauty Is Truly Derived From Our Imperfections......OUR IMPERFECTIONS MAKE US IMPERFECTLY PERFECT....JUST THE WAY WE ARE

TODAY I WOKE UP LOOKED IN THE MIRROR & SAW BEAUTY!!!! Whatever Minor Insecurity and Or Flaw You Have TODAY I pray that you see the BEAUTY that Resonates on the inside & outside of you. YOU'RE BEAUTIFUL Just The Way YOU ARE... GOD MADE NO MISTAKES WHEN HE CREATED YOU!

JOURNAL #10

"It didn't matter that she fell apart, what mattered most was how she put herself back together"
-Unknown

It is my prayer that we ALL realize the imperative significance in SEEING Ourselves....Because Once We See Ourselves We Won't Except Anyone or Anything That Doesn't See Us As Close To How God Sees Us As Possible....

YOU DONT HAVE TO BE "PERFECT" TO BE LOVED PROPERLY & USED BY GOD....OUR IMPERFECTIONS MAKE US WHO WE ARE & OUR HEART DICTATES THE DIRECTION IN WHICH WE ARE GOING (DIVINE DESTINY)!!!!

So today I challenge YOU To LOVE YOU, Love Every Ounce of Your Being!! The Imperfections, the Mistakes, the Vulnerability etc.... Because GOD DOES NOT CALL THE "PERFECT" & OR QUALIFIED.....HE QUALIFIES THE CALLED

JOURNAL #11

Recently I went through a drastic battle it affected me in a major way. I'm talking mentally, physically & spiritually....It was a constant battle between darkness (depression), and light (happiness/freedom)....It was me all alone having to make a decision to either allow myself to stay in a dark place OR shake IT off like the Victor that I am & continue to walk towards & shine the light that God has given me. And If I can be transparent w/you (transparency=freedom for others) for a moment I'll Admit I was Confused, Lost, Empty...I Literally Felt Nothing...All I could think & Say Was "Lord Please Help Me To Get Out Of This Space/Feeling" Whatever IT Was.... IT Was knocking me off my square disrupting the program & standing in the path of my destiny (the enemy smh)....Night after Night Went by & All I Could Do Was Cry Out To God To be honest In Those Moments I Felt Like He didn't Hear Me/Wasn't Listening BUT I WAS WRONG.... He heard my cry, he caught EVERY Tear, He filled that emptiness with wholeness & Brought ME BACK!!! That Feeling Oh IT Went Away SO IM HERE TO TELL YOU WHATEVER Your IT May Be Known And Or Unknown....Caused By The Enemy Or Simply Life Trials/Tribulations.... God SEES, He KNOWS, & He Hears ...NO MATTER HOW HARD IT GETS (No matter What your IT may be) OR HOW EMPTY YOU MAY FEEL ALWAYS SEEK HIM....When You're feeling worthy & when you're feeling Unworthy SEEK HIM & I CAN GUARANTEE YOU HE WILL ANSWER!!!! NEVER LOOSE SIGHT OF YOU....YOUR DESTINY IS WAITING ON YOU GOD HAS A Beyond Peculiar PLAN/PURPOSE FOR YOU & YOUR LIFE.

JOURNAL #12

Baby Girl You Are A Young Woman With BIG Dreams & Not Only Are They BIG BUT They Are GOD-GIVEN Dreams (& gifts)....NEVER Allow Others To Minimize Your Gift....You Continue To Maximize Your GOD/ Dreams/Gifts & FAITH!!!! 1Corinthians 2:9

JOURNEY #13

#Perspective...... We Attract What We Are Ready For. Life is all about your view in which you choose to see things. I would say the way in which you choose to see "certain" things but I believe it's imperative that our view on LIFE as a whole shapes not only our NOW but Our FUTURE. I've come to the realization that when one door closes celebrate it because that just means that God is in the midst of opening another one. He always knows what's best for us, more than we will ever know for ourselves.

JOURNAL #14

GOD HAS YOU EXACTLY WHERE HE WANTS YOU!!!! At times we get so caught up in what we could of done or should've done....Not realizing that we belong to him (GOD) AND HE HAS YOU RIGHT WHERE HE WANTS YOU IN THE PALM OF HIS HAND.....Be Blessed Love Bugs & Let's Make This Year COUNT.

JOURNAL #15

You've been heartbroken and so have I now we're both afraid to give love a try......She hurt you, and he hurt me...I understand it's hard to let go of those memories....Starting over is not a breeze....But all I ask is that you trust in me....Trust & believe I'm scared too...I can't begin to express how I feel when I'm around you...I open my mouth, & I try to speak, but for some reason your very presence makes me weak.....I know I'm not what you're used to & that's ok, I know you've never experienced love in such an intense yet TRUTHFUL way....IDC About what you lack, AUTHENTICITY is what my heart attracts.

JOURNAL #16

This Young Woman Here.....Has Stepped Into A New Dimension....She's GOD APPROVED.....& Works Her Beyond Peculiar Lane So Effortlessly..... Remember The Face, Remember The Smile & Remember The Name.... In A World Of So Many Talented & Beautiful Human Beings, She Chooses To Remain HERSELF......

Oh & S.N. To All My Ladies FOCUS ON GOD, YOU & YOUR DREAMS.......Don't Let These Men Half Love You & NEVER Settle & ALWAYS REMEMBER....

Forgiveness doesn't have to guarantee a second chance.

Know who YOU Are & Know What You DESERVE ....NEVER Trip over These Dudes That Would Be Absurd!

JOURNAL #17

Do You Believe In Second Chances? OR Do You Believe In Love?
Is A Second Chance A Derived Action Of Love?
A 2ND CHANCE
As Days Went by I Missed Your Touch.....
As Weeks went by hmmmm I started not to care so much! THEN "here it comes again"
Night after night I wondered if you were worth a second chance....
If you were worth experiencing my true, pure & authentic love again......
Giving you a second chance?! Does that make me a backup plan?!....
So many memories I can't erase.....
The Way Your Eyes Spoke Every time You Seen My Face.......
Every little moment that constantly replays...... BUT.....Those 2 words you spoke I just can't erase......
NOW Here I Am Torn & A Bit confused....
It's like A Constant Battle between My Mind, My Heart & You
To Be Honest I Don't Know What To do....
I just want To Know If I Give You This 2ND CHANCE,
What Will It Mean to You?!

JOURNAL #18

ALWAYS Keep GOD FIRST & Allow Him To Guide You, Because The Minute You Lose Just A Little Bit Of Focus The Enemy Will Do Everything In His Power To Knock You All The Way Off Track!!!!

JOURNAL #19

LISTEN.....You'll Know When They Really Bout You!!!100 · (Yea I Know That Sounds Real Ratchet BUT It's TRUE)

See the reason why young women are constantly being heartbroken is because they expect TOO MUCH, TOO SOON.....

See Me, I'm A Black Or White Kind Of Girl NO GREY Area In between.....I Promised Myself A LONG Time Ago To Except A Man At Face Value!!!

If He Wants You....He Would Be With You.....If He Likes You....He Will Date You/Spend Time With You....If He Loves You....His ACTIONS Will Show It......If His ACTIONS Changes....There's SOMEONE ELSE..... POINT....BLANK....& PERIOD.

ALWAYS Pay Attention To A Man's Behavior It Speaks Volumes Ladies.... His Actions Alone Will Answer Every Question You Desire To Know..... See My Heartbroken days were OVER 4yrs ago.... Because I've learned to accept A Man at Face Value. DON'T BE BLIND TO THE GAME...Follow Your Instincts Love, & don't Allow Anyone to Play And Or Devalue You Sis You're Worth So Much More Than That

Accept NOTHING Less Than Gods Best.

JOURNAL #20

Thank you for loving me in ways I'd never imagine....Thank you for helping to awake the gifts in me I thought I'd lost......Your presence alone ignites dreams & starts a fire for visions.......God knew EXACTLY what he was doing when he sent you.....MY KING, MY ANSWERED PRAYER TO ALL THINGS.

JOURNAL #21

Sometimes We Just Need to STOP, TAKE A DEEP BREATH, OPEN OUR EARS & TALK TO GOD FOR A MOMENT

Then & ONLY THEN Will We Realize Everything Will Be Just Fine In Fact Everything IS Just Fine!!!! #Jeremiah 33:3

JOURNAL #22

TODAY, it is my prayer that we guard our HEARTS, MINDS, BODIES, & SOULS From DISTRACTIONS.

DISTRACTIONS DEFINITION I:

A thing that prevents someone from giving full attention to something else.

DISTRACTIONS DEFINITION 2:

Extreme agitation of the mind or emotions.

After reading this note It Is my prayer That God opens your eyes & awakens you to the many distractions in your life that are known and unknown.... WHY? Because It Hinders Us From Fulfilling Our GOD Given Destiny.... Distractions Throw You Off Course... Have You Ever Used The GPS & Out Of Nowhere It Takes You All Out The Way Of Reaching Your Destination (that's what the enemy does in our lives ESPECIALLY when we aren't paying attention) You Could Be Close To Your Destination THEN Here Comes DISTRACTIONS....Now It Is Imperative That We Understand The Different Forms Of Distractions As It Pertains To Our Personal Lives.... Certain Things That Distract My Friends, Won't Distract Me....You See The Enemy Is Playing For Keeps And Thinks He's Slick He Will Use People, and or things that he knows will Take Full Force Of Your Attention (Gods Purpose/Plan For Your Life) The enemy's Ultimate Goal Is To STOP You From Reaching Your God-Given Destiny. And All While He Is Trying To Throw You Off Focus, We'll Find Ourselves Openly Allowing Him To ABUSE our Attention...Better Yet We Will Unknowingly Began To Abuse Someone Else's Attention Due To Our Unawareness Of Detour..... So TODAY I want To Leave You With This, YOUR ATTENTION Has A Cost & That Cost Is YOUR DESTINY.

Allow God To Be The Operator Of Your GPS Because His Detours Are Just Small Stops For Fuel. The enemy's Are Distractions That Takes Us All Out The Way Of Our Destiny.

JOURNAL #23

I'll admit, I Really Dig you & I Don't Know Why...Maybe It's The WILDNESS Of Your Touch That Matches The PURITY Of Mine's.

JOURNAL #24

"There's NOTHING More Dangerous Than A Girl Who Has Learned Her Worth"....

& God Has Appointed Me To Help Awaken The Authenticity & GOD-Fidence That Lives On The Inside Of ALL The Beautiful Young Women I Come Across! & I Will Do Just That!!! This Here Is For ANY Young Woman/ Woman That Comes Across This Love Note

Baby Girl, You Are BEAUTIFUL JUST THE WAY YOU ARE.....God Made NO Mistakes When He Created You....KNOW YOUR WORTH & THEN ADD TAX.....Walk Boldly & UNAPOLOGETICALLY In Who GOD Has Created YOU To Be, Even If It Unintentionally Makes Others Feel Uncomfortable Shine That Beyond Peculiar Light Of Yours.

JOURNAL #25

I just want to give you a love that you've never experienced. That love that you're afraid of ...THE LOVE you feel that you don't deserve...a love that shows YOU YOUR TRUE WORTH....See all this time I thought it was me that you didn't see. But in reality, you can't see yourself. But I SEE YOU.....I FEEL YOU....I PRAY FOR YOU.....I LOVE YOU!!! So forgive me for charging your heart for what you can't see, if you don't truly love you how can you truly love me? In order for you to know my worth, you have to know yours first.

I pray that one day you begin to love w/o restrictions.

You know that I would NEVER hurt you, it's time for you to trust your intuition.

JOURNAL #26

Every step you take I'll be right beside you......Every move you make I'll be right behind you.....every Trimble you experience I'll be there to catch you!!! No matter the circumstance I'm here w/you.

JOURNAL #27

NOTE TO SELF: Certain things are worth waiting for & I just so happen to be one of them.

JOURNAL #28

I just want to show you the love you deserve...... I want to show you that I'm not like all these "other" girls.....I want you to experience a love you've never seen.......TRUE, PURE, AUTHENTIC LOVE......YUP, That's Me.

JOURNAL #29

It's ok they're not used to your kind.....their use to a face full of makeup so that you're hard to recognize.......what is standards a foreign language of some kind?.....BUT one day soon you'll be recognized......RECOGNIZED For WHO YOU ARE....He Will grasp your authenticity even from a far........ "Please babe stay true to who you are" because amongst all this darkness you're the shining star".

JOURNAL #30

Some people "WANT" You......Then There Are Those That DESERVE you it's Imperative That We Know the Difference!!!

NOTE TO HUBBY: I Can't Wait To Love You Beyond What Words Can Express.....For You To Hold Me & Take Away All Of Life's Stress.....Of Course, It Won't Be Perfect There Will Be Some Test.....BUT.....I'm Always Down To Fight For Gods ABSOLUTE BEST.....Which is & Will Be YOU!

JOURNAL #31

What Do You See When You Look At Me (When You Think Of Me)? My
Mind Always wonders...Do You Think That You're not enough?!..... Or
Am I Just Too Much?.... For Some Reason, I'm So Infatuated With Your
Touch....For Some Reason, I Know There's More In Store For Us.

JOURNAL #32

L♥VE......Every night isn't always great....the fear of never having you constantly replay's..... Maybe they're right.... "It's too good to be true"..... "There is no man that will WAIT & Truly love you for you".......But see that's the statement I refuse to believe & that's the statement I REFUSE to receive.....For I know what GOD has promised me & He is the orchestrator of ALL Things....

JOURNAL #33

I know so much about you yet I don't know exactly who you are.....but it's like I can feel your very presence even from afar.......I pray that I'm able to love you beyond what the eye can see......& that you love me for nothing more & nothing less but for me simply being ME.....words can't express the love that I feel.....to no not of a man....but knowing that he's real.... Imagining your touch just makes me melt inside.......The PURENESS Of your soul connecting w/mines.....The tears of joy that fall down my face in disbelief..... BUT relieved that this moment is finally taken place...Good things come to those that WAIT.......So I'll continue to walk this path of obedience until my chariot awaits!

JOURNAL #34

Sharing our stories is a 2-Way Street...It Unveils the Pain in You While Setting Your Sister, and Or Brother FREE!!!

Listen, I Hate To Rain On Your Little Parade BUT Your Purpose Isn't Even About You, Nor Is It For You.....Our Transparency And Our Gifts/Stories Were Created For The Freedom And Awakening Of Purpose To Those Connected To Our Journey & Voice because you made it through they have gained GOD-Fidence in knowing they can as well.

JOURNAL #35

Sometimes you can Love the RIGHT Person at the WRONG TIME, AND sometimes you can Love the WRONG Person at the RIGHT TIME!!!

JOURNAL #36

I cannot charge you for the way in which you were taught to love, BUT I can set a standard in the way in which you choose to love me.

JOURNAL #37

Let it go sis,
They KNEW better, and they should have DONE Better. STOP charging yourself with the guilt of walking away due to the pain that they have caused.

You CAN NOT allow people residents in your heart Who Don't See You Properly!!!

I showed you who I was & YOU STILL COULDN'T SEE.....I gave you all my love & you STILL COULDN'T SEE.....I unknowingly set aside my beliefs & you STILL COULDN'T SEE.....I was an open book & you STILL DIDN'T READ....

I will always love you but I had to choose me, I can no longer allow people access to linger in my life who don't SEE ME PROPERLY.

JOURNAL #38

You don't have time to teach someone how to LOVE you!!!
You don't have time to teach someone how to BELIEVE in you!!!
AND you don't have time to teach someone how to SEE you!!!
NO, YOU SIMPLY DO NOT HAVE TIME FOR THAT

YES, the Word of God tells us, "with all thy getting get understanding" (Proverbs 4:7). HOWEVER, if we are honest with ourselves, we'll see and realize that we are holding on to things and people God has commanded us to let go of a long time ago.

Sweetheart now you know there is NOTHING else left to discuss. We prolong the process of moving on and removing people from our lives because, in all honesty, we don't want to let go, BUT today it's not about what we "want" to do. Our feelings will lead us back into the bad situationships that God has freed us from. TODAY, we will choose OURSELVES and most importantly THE WILL OF GOD for our lives.....

Listen, God is a jealous God BUT he is also a gentleman who gives each of us free will. Let's not abandon his covering (asset), with our desperation (liability).

LET GO of that thing.

JOURNAL #39

As a little girl, you always dream of one day BECOMING a WOMAN......
You dream with such innocent and pure intentionality, not knowing the
life and journey that lies ahead. As time and age progress you begin to
realize that part of becoming a woman involves GROWING. Growth
is that one part of life that takes you by complete surprise because it
forces you to deal with this beautiful thing called life, and the trials and
tribulations that unknowingly come with it. Growth is that moment where
fear is present BUT your Faith in God Prevails. There's something special
about experiencing life through the lens of a woman. There is so much
POWER that is released through the transparency of sharing our stories.
As a woman when we share our stories it is a 2 way street it unveils
the pain in you while also setting your sister free. Being a woman is all
about BECOMING, GROWING, AND EVOLVING Into the precious
yet POWERFUL jewel that God has created you to be, and doing it with
GOD-FIDENCE unapologetically. Being a woman is all about staying
true to who God has called you to be. Shining your Beyond Peculiar light
authentically, and effortlessly while encouraging other beauties to do the
same.

My name is Racquel Cooney (a.k.a. thee peculiar one) and I was once a
precious caterpillar, now I am ready to EVOLVE into A Beautiful Butterfly.
Sis, Are you ready to EVOLVE and Soar with Me?

JOURNAL #40

Situationship-
/ˌsiCHəˈwāSH(ə)n/ SHip/

*Wanting RELATIONSHIP benefits (on your own time & expense) without actually being in a relationship.

* A Placebo masking itself as a formative relationship.

1. This Massive Grey Area, a Place Where Black & White NEVER Exist.

Sis, Listen to me GET OUT, RUN OUT, CRY OUT Whatever Route You Take Make Sure You EXIT OUT Of That Situation-ship....It Serves You No Benefits...It Has Become A Liability To Your Life As Oppose To A Beneficial Asset....It Has Broken The Mirror In Which You See Yourself, And Has Caused Your Vision Of Self To Result In Broken/Clouded Judgement. No Matter How Much It Hurts, Or How Much You Love That Individual TODAY YOU MUST Make The Decision To CHOOSE & LOVE YOU.

Make This Deceleration With Me:
I WILL NOT ACCEPT NOTHING LESS THAN GOD'S ABSOLUTE BEST FOR MY LIFE.

S.N. Don't Worry He And Or She (For My Fellas) Will Be Alright And It Is My Prayer That They Understand.....

"I Don't Want you to be angry w/me, it's just that I have to be loved the RIGHT way I can no longer live in the GREY!!!"

JOURNAL #41

Statistics state that the number 1 thing people search for is LOVE.....only if we knew that we don't have to search for ANYTHING or ANYONE because THE ONLY LOVE WE NEED comes from the only true & Indestructible LOVE there Is, JESUS CHRIST.

We don't have to look for it in terrible relationships, friendships, situation-ships, sex, abuse NONE of IT!!! The ultimate act of Love & Ultimate Sacrifice Was Displayed and Given to ALL OF US...For ALL OF US ON THE CROSS.

Walking away from someone that you care about and have grown to love is not by any means easy. As a matter of fact it is extremely painful, BUT In life we have to make decisions for the betterment of ourselves and even for those in which we choose to walk away from.

ALWAYS Remember The moment you begin to question whether or not you deserve better 9 times out of 10 YOU PROBABLY DO (That pertains to ANYTHING In Life). Your time and your energy is an Investment, and it's something that you will NEVER be able to get back. Place your energy into those people and things that SEE YOU PROPERLY, and those that UNSELFISHLY give because they GENUINELY care. Invest your time into things and people that consider it a gift to even be graced by your presence (as opposed to taking advantage of it)....

RECIPROCITY IS IMPERATIVE As It Relates To Your Life & God-Given Purpose.

What We Allow In Our Lives, Displays A Direct Reflection Of The Way In Which We See Ourselves.....See Yourself Properly, My Love.

JOURNAL #42

GOD-FIDENCE: An Undoubtedly Amount of Confidence That Comes Straight From GOD!!!!

When You Simply Just Have "Confidence", there will always be room for self-doubt because you rely on yourself, BUT when we seek and withhold Confidence that comes from GOD.....We rediscover this amazing asset that radiates from within.....GOD-FIDENCE!!!!

Bad company corrupts good character!!!... YES, WE ALL Are Purpose-Filled BUT Not everyone Is PURPOSE LED.....PURPOSE LED Is The Action & Initiative To Actively Be Obedient To The Life & Gift God Has called you to & placed down on the inside of you.

Remember, It's Always The Good Ones That Get Caught Up....Being In The Wrong Place At The Wrong Time.....The Enemy Knows The Power You Have On The Inside & Over Your Life......He Isn't A Gentlemen He Doesn't Want To See Us Win. His ULTIMATE Goal In Life Is For Us To FAIL...... BUT On This Day, In This Moment I Stand In The Gap For Some, & Pray Beside Others That Unknowingly & Knowingly Are In An Atmosphere Or Relationships (friendships, situation-ships) That The Enemy Is Trying To Subliminally Use To Ruin Gods Ultimate Plan For Our Lives, And The Souls That Our Destiny/Testimonies Are Attach To......GOD BREAK ANY RELATIONSHIP THAT IS NOT LIKE YOU & GIVE US THE WILL POWER TO OBEY YOUR VOICE AND FOLLOW THAT POWERFUL GIFT THAT EACH OF US HAVE....OUR INSTINCTS!!!

JOURNAL #43

You have EVERY Right to Ruunnnn from ANY Individual Who Lacks Respect, Support, Honesty, Pure Intentionality & Reciprocity as It Pertains to YOU & YOUR LIFE!!!

Your self-worth & YES even your very own existence is worth far more than ANY individual who is currently displaying those actions......NEVER Allow People Access Into Your Life, Or Access To LINGER In Your Life Who Is Unable & UNWILLING To See You Properly.

JOURNAL #44

When you are dating someone it is important that they RESPECT and VALUE YOU......A man who doesn't RESPECT/VALUE you will NEVER be an asset to you or your life. RESPECT/VALUE is exemplified and demonstrated through honest & pure gestures......

*When you are with him you should feel safe.

*When you are with him chivalry should be ALIVE and in FULL effect!!!

To society, it may be "dead" BUT with you, it should always remain alive, and a NECESSITY.

*When you both are out in public he should NEVER demonstrate actions that make you feel less than while making another woman feel more than.

Sis, ultimately we know the difference between RESPECT and DISRESPECT and there should be NO thin line between the two.

BLACK or WHITE....NO GREY In Between.

JOURNAL #45

Sometimes we have to reluctantly remove people from our lives so that we won't go back to the place, habits, and routines that God freed and delivered us from once before. Yea I know it hurts, yea they may think it's selfish BUT Your God-ordained purpose is far more important....reaching and being ALL that God has called you to be and Receiving ALL that God has in store is IMPERATIVE......NOTHING ELSE matters more than walking and living in the TRUE FULFILLMENT Of Who God has purposed you to be. This world needs you, someone here on planet earth has a Precise NEED & HUNGER and the only way they can be fulfilled is through the transparency and testimony in which only you can offer.

It's not about being selfish or inconsiderate of others it's just that this season of my life is very significant and MY DESTINY is right in my grasp, I can't afford to waste my time and energy on anything and or anyone who will ultimately deter me from fulfilling and receiving What God has in store for me.

Those of you reading this shouldn't either. Time & energy is something none of us will EVER get back....use your time & energy wisely.

JOURNAL #46

There are those who date just to simply date....Then They're those who apply intentionality behind their dating.....It is IMPERATIVE that we know the difference.

Time is something that none of us can get back and I don't mean to sound arrogant and or selfish BUT when there is a calling and assignment on your life no matter the magnitude, "Games" & UNCERTAINTY IS NOT APART OF THE PLAN AND It WILL NOT be a part of the plan for my life...

Why? Because God has bigger plans for me on my agenda, and being insignificant or a second priority is not about to be checked ✓ off!!!

MY list consumes GOD, Authentic Love, purpose, drive, PURE intentionality, and last but certainly not least reciprocity and yours should too.

JOURNAL #47

There are those who live their lives to simply exist.....Then there are those who live their lives with GOD ORDAINED Purpose because they know life is bigger than their very own existence.....There is a significant difference between the two....I want you to place your hand upon your chest you feel that heartbeat? It's called PURPOSE, GOD ORDAINED PURPOSE..... Today I challenge you to get up and walk and work towards your destiny.... You're waiting on God, BUT God is waiting on YOU!!! Do your best and I can guarantee you He will do the rest. Activate your faith, today your destiny awaits you my love.

JOURNAL #48

Sis, Listen.....Learn How To Except A Man At Face Value......Their Actions
Are A True Indication Of Their Feelings....

JOURNAL #49

Today I had to make a decision and come to the realization that I can't SAVE you. Nor can I unknowingly force salvation onto you either......At this moment I have to Save MYSELF, because I find myself losing sight of who God has created/ordained me to be in hopes that I can help you reach the full potential and manifestation of who you "COULD" be, and your God-given destiny....

Sis, it is my prayer that you never lose yourself for the sake of saving someone else. THAT'S GOD'S JOB, Allow God to be God. He's God ALL by himself, he doesn't need your help. Allow GOD to be the author of your Love story.

2 Corinthians 6:14 Mark 10:9

JOURNAL #50

Sis, I want you to meditate, digest, and comprehend this next statement....

We (You) can't expect a man to do for us (you) what he is unable to do for himself!!! If he doesn't pray how can he pray/cover you? If he doesn't dream how can he believe and support your dreams? If he doesn't value commitment how do you expect him to be committed to you? If he doesn't believe In Jesus Christ how do you expect Christ to be in the center of your relationship? It's absurd right?! Why must we even place ourselves in the position of indecisiveness? Indecisiveness & compromise of God's will, will NEVER lead you down the aisle. It leads you straight to destruction. Yes it hurts, yes you love him BUT you and I both know its Gods way because your way leads to heartache & destruction.

JOURNAL #51

SIS, Let Me Explain Something To You.

NEVER, I REPEAT NEVER Let ANYONE Disrespect You. No Boy, No Girl, No Woman AND ESPECIALLY NO MAN!!!! What You Allow Becomes A Habit & If Disrespect Is In The Mist I Need For You To KILL It RIGHT NOW....GIVE RESPECT & ALWAYS BE SURE THAT IT IS RECIPROCATED. Why?! Because Home Girl Don't Play That & With Disrespect Comes Dismissal....So, It's There Choice & They Better Choose Wisely.

JOURNAL #52

A man who values you will NEVER Disrespect you, nor will he let another woman disrespect you.....The keyword was VALUE. If He Does Either Of Those Things, You Have A Problem On Your Hands, And It Needs To Be Solved, Either By Making Him Aware Of His Actions In Hopes That He Will Understand And Change, OR By Removing Him From Your Life, Because Those Who Love & Value You Can't Possibly Allow Disrespect To Occupy And Take Up Residence Within Your Relationship.

Where there is DISRESPECT there should also be DISMISSAL. NEVER allow disrespect to occupy and take residence in your life.

JOURNAL #53

The worst thing is having to let go of someone you've grown to love......
because it hinders you from loving the way God intends for us to Love.
Great things come to those who WAIT.

JOURNAL #54

I'm not obsessed with my gifts and talents..... I'm Obsessed with GODS WILL.

JOURNAL #55

It's amazing how much we sacrifice daily for those we love.....how many times have we said to ourselves and those around us "He or She's lucky I love them because if not I would of been......" "I know that I shouldn't but I love him it's hard", or "I want to say no, but I love them and if I do I'm afraid that I'll lose them".......GOD LOVES US so much that he gave US HIS ONLY Begotten Son.....JESUS LOVES Us so, that he gave HIS LIFE.....& We have the audacity to sacrifice God's will, word, and obedience because we "LOVE" Someone......The Only love that deserves to be obtained & sacrificed is THE LOVE OF JESUS ....LOVE AS CHRIST LOVES....If it doesn't represent & correspond with Christ-like love it isn't worth the sacrifice. God's will and His way is EVERYTHING......Without Alignment of His LOVE & WILL, we'll lose EVERYTHING!!!!

JOURNAL #56

Energy, Vibes, Time, & LOVE Should Be RECIPROCATED.......You CAN NOT Live Your Life In Continuous GIVE, GIVE, and GIVE Mode To Those Who Don't Reciprocate/GIVE In Return. We should NEVER allow ourselves to give to the point in which we never RECEIVE in Return.... ENERGY, VIBES, TIME, & LOVE Is EXCHANGEABLE.....

Times Out For Giving ALL Of You & Others Declaring No Exchanges OR Refunds.

JOURNAL #57

Today I challenge you to redefine your circle and evaluate your desires.....
Are they in alignment with God's will, plan, and purpose for your life?
Comfortability is the enemy of purpose & fulfillment. NEVER Allow
someone to gain continuous access to you and your life just because you
are "use" to them being there. Some people have an expiration date & just
like food once it expires we have to throw it out. It can no longer feed us
if we allow ourselves to consume expired food we will cause damage to
our bodies....as to our Destiny. Throw away what is no longer beneficial &
good for you, so that you can make (have) room for all of the great things
that should consume you.

JOURNAL #58

One of the most dangerous things you can do is begin to fall in love w/ someone who doesn't know how to love properly. It hurts to say, but it will NEVER work. You can't teach someone how to love you. The only person who can fix that problem is GOD.....Sometimes you just have to LITERALLY LET GO Of that person & Let God Cultivate their heart to Love Properly, The Way He intends for us to Love.....They May have missed out on Loving You, but at least He (God) will have guided & transformed them for the next Good thing they are blessed to come across.

JOURNAL #59

In life, things may happen to us, BUT GOD stands FOR US!!!! He makes EVERYTHING Beautiful!

JOURNAL #60

Brokenness is CHOICE, HEALING is a process, BUT FORGIVENESS &
WHOLENESS ARE THEE ONLY OPTIONS!!!

JOURNAL #61

Ultimately our blessings are tied into the way in which we treat others…if today was your last day here on earth, how would you help to release the burden off of someone's life with your everyday acts of love? If you desire a life of abundance, blessings & favor ask yourself; how am I treating others on a day to day basis? God does not bless our acts of mess only our acts of bless(ed).

JOURNAL #62

If you've never experienced depression don't speak on it....If you've never experienced abuse & or verbal abuse don't speak on it... if you've never experienced a specific illness be it mental or physical don't speak on it! 9 times out of 10 when people are in these states they don't need your "opinion" they simply just need your presence. Learn how to be there for others without contaminating their current state even more.

JOURNAL #63

Don't allow what you see to dictate who you are... You have the power to change your narrative & to speak life over your life!!!

JOURNAL #64

Wholeness is A CHOICE....Don't allow BROKENNESS to be an option!!!

JOURNAL #65

Have you ever had a freedom relapse?! If So It's Ok I Want You To Say This Prayer Out loud To God & Yourself.

Lord forgive me for inviting/tampering with things (and at times people) that are a disruption to my ultimate FREEDOM. Give me the strength I need to stay the healing & freedom course without RELAPSING to the things and or people whose ultimate agenda is to keep me bound. Allow me to remember who you've created me to be & to dwell in KNOWING that HEALING is a process but WHOLENESS is thee only option. Help me to forgive ME even when the relapse is present & the journey ahead is uncertain. Allow me to rest in the certainty of YOU & The ULTIMATE Calling upon My Life.....Forgive me for my unbelief in self & at times due to my fear, my unbelief in you.

JOURNAL #66

Matthew 5:16

I've never claimed to be JESUS; However, I WILL do my absolute BEST to be/become an exemplification of him...That's what being a Christian is all about!

JOURNAL #67

REPEAT AFTER ME:

I will NOT hold onto anyone & or anything whose actions indicate that they don't want to hold on to me. NEVER beg for a position in someone's life…We MUST LEARN TO VALUE OURSELVES!

We've FOUGHT & CRIED for positions that weren't ASSIGNED to us. We WILL NOT be a victim of our own destruction. LOVE YOURSELF ENOUGH!!!

JOURNAL #68

Some People Can Claim to Love God, But Not Love the GOD IN YOU... & Depending Upon How Imperative The Relation & Position Of The Individual It Can Truly Hurt Deeply BUT Here's The PLOT TWIST.... It's Impossible To Claim Gods Love But Dislike A Form Of His Love No Matter The Magnitude Or The Vessel In Which He Chooses To Use.... All In All, CONTINUE To Be ALL That God Has Called You To Be & Act Upon His Voice. EVEN IF It Unintentionally Makes Others Feel Uncomfortable!!!

JOURNAL #69

You desire to know if he truly loves you? Ok, here it is Sis it's simple....

- He SAYS It Verbally—-SHOWS It DAILY
- He PRAYS For You!

A Man's Love for a Woman Is Primarily Based on Those Two Simplistic Gestures. If A Man Has A Problem Uttering The Words "I Love You" & He Doesn't Even Mention You In His Daily Prayers To God..... THERE'S Your Answer!

JOURNAL #70

The heart of someone working towards the FULL manifestation of WHOLENESS Is NOT COMPATIBLE with the heart of a BROKEN Individual that dwells on STAYING that way.

JOURNAL #71

No matter how relatable our lanes are in comparison to others, there is still our own SPECIFIC Approach in which God REQUIRES each of us to fulfill.

JOURNAL #72

It's imperative for us to demonstrate love often; loving the woman beside you In Sisterhood & EVEN RELATIONSHIP Terror.

JOURNAL #73

If you're someone who feels that not everyone has purpose...... you lack the FULL KNOWING OF GOD & WHO HE IS!! God creates EVERYTHING with intent & PURPOSE; Our Heartbeats Are an Indicator of That.

Jeremiah 29:11 Is An Indicator Of That!!! Go READ IT FOR YOURSELF!

JOURNAL #74

So many times as humans especially us "*millennials*" if something doesn't LOOK Like or resemble what **WE'RE** used to we **DEVALUE** it; & that must change. In order to fully **VALUE** LIFE as well as OTHER'S, we have to be open to the ways & beings of life that come in forms OUTSIDE OF OURSELVES & what we are used to.

JOURNAL #75

Some people Were raised on *Love* others on *Survival;* it's a DRASTIC difference & perception of life. HOWEVER, BOTH Ways of LIVING produce different ways of LOVING and we MUST be ok in learning the love languages of others. Not everyone has the same prescription of vision but in every dose, RESPECT must be given.

JOURNAL #76

Often times When people don't know who you are or what God-ordained Purpose really is they misinterpret the calling upon your life!! Walk your lane with GOD-Fidence anyway.

JOURNAL #77

We have to learn to listen to God's voice there's no way we can claim that we listen to him & our actions towards others indicate otherwise. If we truly listen to God's voice we should be speaking with kindness, treating with kindness, showing respect, etc... You CAN NOT Claim to love God & treat people poorly!!

JOURNAL #78

Just Because The WANT Is There Doesn't Mean The DESERVE Is There.....There Is A Thin Line Between "SAYING"..... "SHOWING" AND "SEEING"!!! Who Are You Allowing To Have Access To Your Heart? Whoever Holds Your Heart MUST SEE Your Heart And See YOU As Close To How God Sees You As Possible.

JOURNAL #79

When You Love God Properly You Love People Properly.

JOURNAL #80

If you can't take God's hand and walk with him.....You definitely can't take mines and walk with me. Equally yoked partnerships are imperative.

JOURNAL #81

To Acknowledge Something That Bothers You And Or Makes You Feel Uneasy Is NOT An Act Of Being Argumentative It's Literally Called COMMUNICATION......When Someone Doesn't Allow You To Express Yourself; & Then Tries To Guilt Trip You Into Thinking You're Wrong For Wanting To Do So THAT'S Called MANIPULATION....Manipulation In One Of Its Highest Forms. You MUST Allow Those You Love To Express Themselves It's A Form Of HEALTHY Communication.....Blocking That Expression Is A Form Of GUILT.

JOURNAL #82

YOU Set The Standard/Tone Of How Someone Talks To You; The More People Destruct You With Their Tongue The More DAMAGED You Become. You Give Someone An Inch They're Going to go a mile.... STANDARDS, Never Too Late To Activate. LOVE Has Standards, Relationships, Friendships, Business-ships HAVE STANDARDS That's How You Thrive Through Them All....By Communicating & Executing Them Through The Lens Of Love.

JOURNAL #82

It doesn't matter what type of dysfunctions and suffering MOST people go through....That IS NOT An indication that you have to accept and or put up with it too. This universe unfortunately operates predominately on SURVIVAL & BROKENNESS ......THAT DOES NOT Place ME In A Position To Be Willing To Just Accept That As Well....NO! LOVE & WHOLENESS Is What Truly Brings About Strength.....You see, SURVIVAL & BROKENNESS is the COWARD "feel bad for me" way out.....NO, You MUST HEAL! HEAL! HEAL! There Is Absolutely NOTHING Cute & or Attractive about being broken and trying to drag others into brokenness with you.

JOURNAL #83

Who God Has Created/Called You To Be; Should NEVER Offend The Person You Love.

JOURNAL #84

It's Called "Partners in Purpose" For a Reason, They Understand Your Gift/Calling AND You UNDERSTAND THERE'S. You Embark On The Journey Of Life TOGETHER In Your Own Distinctive Yet PECULIAR Way(s).

JOURNAL #85

✦ I Declare Today That Your Abundance Is In Your Perseverance ✦

Don't Allow Your Lack Of Resources To Limit Your Amount Of Action....
God Will Bless What You ALREADY HAVE, And Through Your
Perseverance Your Hand Will Began To Overflow.

"Use What You've Got To Get What You Want" If We Just Become More
Faithful Over A FEW Things He Will Make Us Ruler Of MANY Things.

Matthew 25:23

JOURNAL #86

The number one thing I will NOT Tolerate From ANYONE IS DISRESPECT.....If Someone Chooses To Disrespect You It Is An Indication That They Don't VALUE You & No Matter What You've Done Or What You've Been To Someone And Or There Personal Perception(s) Of You. DISRESPECT SHOULD NEVER BE THERE OUTCOME OF ACTION.

Disrespect= an intentional action to deliberately hurt an individual.

JOURNAL #87

WHOLENESS Is NOT Compatible To BROKENNESS

JOURNAL #88

People can only LOVE From the Perspective in Which They Were Loved Themselves. You'd Be Surprised How Many Individuals Feel As If Verbal Abuse & Blame(age).......Is Love Because That's What Was Once Given To Them.....The Differentiation Of Being Raised On LOVE V.S. SURVIVAL Is IMPERATIVE.

JOURNAL #89

Where Purpose, Passion, & Pursuit Meet!!

JOURNAL #90

God & I hold the key to my success.....& with his POWER & My OBEDIENCE I am willing to unlock, create, & breakthrough doors & realms of never seen nor obtained opportunities.

JOURNAL #91

You cannot commune or allow others access to you who don't see you properly......We ALL require a certain amount of RESPECT & VALUE in life and it must be shown and Reciprocated. NEVER Answer to & or engulf yourself in things that are a disgrace to who God has created/called & NAMED you To Be. We Are Children of God WE MUST ACT like it & ANSWER like it; don't allow ANY Individual to mishandle you. God has set the standard....Now abide by it and walk through it properly. You are a jewel 💎 & must be seen and treated as such!

JOURNAL #92

☐STOP ....Stop Worrying About Telling "Your Side" Of The Story! When Your Heart & Intentions Are PURE & You've Done Right By Other's There Is Absolutely NO REASON To FRET Or PROVE ANYTHING.... FOR GOD SEES AND HE KNOWS ALL THINGS.....People May Be Able To Lie To Others BUT ONE THING IS FOR CERTAIN They Can't Lie To GOD AND We ALL Have To Answer To God When It's ALL SAID & DONE!!

JOURNAL #93

If it's not GOD ....

I DONT WANT IT

If it doesn't resemble GOD

I DONT NEED IT

If It Claims To Love God; But It's Actions Display Different.....

I DEFINITELY DONT DESIRE IT....

Moral of the story at this point in life WITH ALL THINGS..... If it isn't GOD I'm Running For My Life Because The Devil Really Thinks He's Slick BUT Nahhhhh .....There's FREEDOM & WHOLENESS Attached to MY LIFE!!!! #Period

JOURNAL #94

Intentionally inflicting pain onto others serves as a sign of brokenness. WHOLE people desire to love on others. BROKEN people desire to watch them bleed.

JOURNAL #95

One thing I've learned in life we can't worry about what others do. YOU'VE got to focus on YOU (YOUR ACTIONS, YOUR HEART, YOUR FLAWS & SHORTCOMINGS THE WAY YOU TREAT & OR TREATED OTHERS) ....YES even when things happen & are done to us and or to our loved ones & friends......Stand on knowing that things may happen TO US BUT GOD Stands FOR US!! & we MUST know this. It's not our job to understand all the time nor to "pay people back". Listen God can handle people better then we can Chileee (in my Granny's voice)..... At the end of this journey, we're held accountable for OURSELVES......

JOURNAL #96

God like gestures are of PURE Intent even in the mist of chaos…

GOD'S VOICE LEADS US TO VICTORY NOT FOLLOWING IT LEADS US TO DESTRUCTION

JOURNAL #97

We as people (the nation, and the world) We HAVE to get it together..... we no longer fear God & it's exemplified by OUR ACTIONS.....How we treat other's, how we disobey his commandments, the way in which we talk to others, how we think that we have "more time". WE HAVE BECOME Numb to the principle of CONSEQUENCES Because God has been so gracious to give us GRACE & because Our Savior is sitting at the right hand of the father fighting on our behalf......

LIFE Is All About 3 Things.....

* GODS PURPOSE FOR OUR LIVES

* HOW WE TREAT OTHERS

* And ULTIMATELY Those Gates

JOURNAL #98

There Are So Many People Who Claim JESUS CHRIST As there Lord & Savior BUT Are Embarrassed To Be In Association Or Publicly Acknowledge That Love (Not Saying You Have To Be All Uptight & PERFECT Because ALL OF US ARE FAR FROM PERFECTION OKAYYYY?!).....BUT....Here's The Thing & I Mean This In The Most HUMBLE & NON-JUDGEMENTAL Way Possible

"If You Can't Take GOD'S Hand In CONFIDENCE And Walk W/ Him.....You DEFINITELY Can't Take My Hand & Walk W/Me" PERRRIIOODDD**!!!!**

JOURNAL #99

You Can Be YOU & STILL LOVE GOD; It Isn't "WACK" What's Wack Is TAKING YOUR LAST breath & Walking Up To Those Gates & NOT GETTING IN.....Now, None of us, by All Means, are NOWHERE NEAR PERFECT Enough To Say "I'm Going To Make It Into Heaven" We All Fall Short DAILY At Times Both Intentionally (KNOWING BETTER) & UN-Intentionally BUT as it pertains to me I Can GUARANTEE You That It Won't Be Because I WAS AFRAID TO ACKNOWLEDGE HIM & or SUPPORT THINGS That Represent Him and it shouldn't be for you either.

🔊 MATTHEW 10:33 🔊

"but whoever denies me before men, I also will deny before my Father who is in heaven."

JOURNAL #100

Choose Who YOU CHOOSE To Fight For Wisely.... (Read That AGAIN; & Allow It To Marinate In Your Spirit) Some Individuals Don't Desire To Be Saved & If Saving Them Ultimately Results In Hurting You The Risk Isn't Worth The Outcome Of The Battle....You CAN NOT Be The Bloody Hero All The Time THAT'S JESUS JOB.....ONLY HIS Blood Can Heal.... You Trying To Protect What Doesn't Require Your Touch Only Breaks Your Heart!!!

It's amazing how we continuously protect the ones we love and have once loved from people, places, and things that they find comfort in...Simply so that they won't be hurt and or destroyed BUT sometimes we must use DISCERNMENT in knowing that everyone doesn't desire to be saved... especially not at YOUR expense.

JOURNAL #101

Have You Ever Felt Undervalued, Overlooked, Underappreciated....
Yes, YOU...The STRONG FRIEND, Strong DAUGHTER, Strong
GIRLFRIEND, Strong MOM, Strong WIFE & Whatever Other Position
You So Effortlessly Fulfill Day To Day....I Just Want You To Know That I
SEE YOU.....You Are LOVED, APPRECIATED & VALUED ...... I Know
That You're Simply TIRED & Yes I'm Aware That It's Not A Physical
Tired, It's Your Mind, Soul, & Heart..... I SEE YOU, I FEEL YOU & I
Understand... CONTINUE To Be Who You Are Even When Others Can't
See, Apologize, Understand, etc....God does...Thank You For Your Act Of
Selflessness; You've Buried Your Feelings For The Protection Of Others....
Don't You Worry, You've Got This!

JOURNAL #102

Words Hurrrttttttt......Be Mindful Of What You Say To The Ones You Love.......You Can Lose Someone Just By The Looseness Of Your Tongue.... Once Words Are Spoken Into The Universe Or Towards An Individual The Damage Is Already Done. There's No Taking Them Back!

JOURNAL #103

I Feel That People Deserve Partners Who Are & Have An "ALL ABOUT YOU" Mentality......Especially Once You Reach A Certain Age & Point In Your Life/Career Etc.....No One Is Perfect, But Be With Someone Who's Going To Love You For Who You Are & Choose YOU Over & Over Again..... Now, I'm Not Saying Accept The Toxic Traits In Individuals And Call That "Love" NO That's TOXICITY NOT HEALTHY !!! #BIGFacts I'm Saying Be With Someone Who Allows You To Simply Be You W/O Having To Feel Guilty For It ESPECIALLY The Parts Of You That Are Positive...No, Life Is NOT A Fairy Tale BUT LIFE Is What You Make It AND YOU Deserve A Love That Doesn't Involve Suffering First To Reach Its Pure Potential.....Your Desire For WHOLENESS/POSITIVITY Shouldn't Offend Anyone If It Does Unfortunately They Desire A Form Of Brokenness (Yea, That Hurts)...You Deserve ALL OR NOTHING IN EVERY SHIP You Have (RelationSHIP, FriendSHIP, BusinessSHIP). In 2020 You're Either ALL IN Or ALL NOTHING (In EVERY Aspect Of My Life) It's A Choice. Choose Wisely.

JOURNAL #104

As Millennials It Is OUR Responsibility To CHANGE The Narrative...... We're What I Like To Call The "Generation Of Blame" Meaning We Have SO MUCH POTENTIAL & GREATNESS Within BUT We Blame Everyone EXCEPT Ourselves; As A Reason & Or "Validation" To Not TAKE ACCOUNTABILITY For Who We Currently Are (EVEN THE UGLY PARTS OF US) & Put Forth The INITIATIVE TO CHANGE...... YES, It Is True For Some Of Us That Those Before Us In Some Way Contributed To Our Current Dysfunctions, Toxicity & Or Flaws...Whether Minute Or Colossal BUT IT'S NOW OUR RESPONSIBILITY AS ADULTS TO CHANGE THAT......

If You Grew Up In A BROKEN Family; & Or Unfortunately Were Never Even Exposed To What A REAL Family Looks Like..... It Is YOUR Responsibility To MAKE SURE That A WHOLE FAMILY Comes From YOU (NO EXCUSES)

I Also Want To Shed Light On INFIDELITY In Our Generation; WE MUST Change That Narrative.....NO MATTER WHAT YOU DO (Occupation) OR WHO YOU ARE (Position Of Power) Ppl. Are Tempted EVERY DAY.....It Is YOUR Responsibility To Choose WHOLENESS For YOUR FAMILY!!!

We All Have Our Own Depictions Of What Love Is....& I'm Not Just Referring To Love Through The Lens Of Relationships BUT LOVE Through The Lens Of Family, Friendship, Acq-uaintance, Ministry, Business, Etc.... Each Of Us Have Our Own LOVE LANGUAGES As Well However, I Am Fully Aware That We Are Required To Love Through The Lens Of Christ.....So, With That Being Said In What Ways Can You Do/Be Better In Terms Of Exemplifying That Love?!....... Because Whether We Want To Believe It Or Not WE ALL WANT TO BE LOVED & RECEIVE LOVE...... BUT We Forget To Be A GIVER Of LOVE & That's IMPERATIVE Because We NEVER Know When It Is Our Last Chance To Exemplify!

JOURNAL #105

When Experiencing A New Life Journey W/Those You Love....You Must Learn To Consider The One's You Love & That Love You In Return AND Remember That It's Not Always About One's Self.....Someone You Love Could Be Suffocating For Freedom, Compassion, Time, Appreciation, Etc.....The Picture Is ALWAYS Bigger Than Ourselves.....Others Are In The Portrait Along With You and It's Imperative To Know That Wanting To Communicate Doesn't Have To Equate To An Act Of Being Argumentative Just Simply Understanding!

JOURNAL #106

This is Just For Those Of Us Who Are PURPOSE-FILLED & Know That Life Is Bigger Than US......This Is For Those Who Desire Leaving A LEGACY Behind....Making God\Jesus Name Great Amongst The Earth & Raising Phenomenal Seeds (Young KINGS & QUEENS 👑) To Do So As Well.....PEEP THIS......

After You've Reached A Certain Age In Life & You're Striving Towards Something Greater Than You....You MUST Surround Yourself With Those Going/Aiming For What Your Heart Desires & ACT AS SUCH........ For Example: If You Desire To Quit Smoking cigarettes 🚬 You SHOULDN'T Surround Yourself W/The Company Of Those Who Are Constantly Smoking Right?! You More Than Likely Will Be Tempted & Find It Harder To Succeed........PUT FORTH THAT SAME EFFORT For What You Desire....ALLOW What You Speak As An Hearts Desire To MATCH What You're Doing As Well As The Company YOU KEEP!

You WANT A FAMILY?! Having Multiple Women/Men & Being Around People Who AREN'T MARRIED Is NOT The Way To Achieve That Desire..... Surround Yourself W/Those Who Have Significant Others/ Families (FAITHFUL ONES)!

You WANT TO START THAT BUSINESS? Being Around People Who Desire To Sit On Their Behinds & Work For Others In A Mediocre "Lane" & Or "Mindset" IS NOT The Way To Put Forth The Effort To ACHIEVE That. Surround Yourself W/Other ENTREPRENEURS!

SIMPLE......Be & Or Work Towards The CHANGE & REFLECTION Of What YOU Speak/Desire.....NO It Won't Be Easy & Or "Cool" To Other's BUT If IT'S GODS WILL, YOU WANT IT, AND You're PURPOSE-FILLED It's WORTH IT ALL!!!

JOURNAL #107

"Don't Just Love Me When You're Not Feeling Yourself Fully.....Love Me Also When You Start To Fully Smell Yourself Again" ....

It's Easy For Friends, Family, & Significant Other(s) To Love You Through That Personal Trenches Season BUT The Real Action Of Love Comes When The Manifestation/Glow Season Begins Again.....LOVE Yours AT ALL COST.... & AT ALL TIMES...In ALL SEASONS Of Your Life.

JOURNAL #108

If the humiliation was public.....the reconciliation should be just as LOUD
#Love Yours or #LoseYours The Ball Is Always In One's Own Court.....
Time To Shoot Or Pass The Ball!

JOURNAL #109

Hello Black King & Queen...I Want You To Know That MENTAL HEALTH Is Extremely Imperative/Significant.....AND......

Verbal/Emotional Abuse IS REAL...Seek The Help & Guidance If You Feel The Need & Urge To Do So NEVER Allow Society To Make You Feel That You're Crazy For Wanting Change & Betterment For Yourself...THAT IS What Therapy/ Consultation Is For...Don't Lose Your Mind Nor Your Self Based Upon The Opinion Of Someone Else. GET THE HELP THAT IS NEEDED......Your HEALING, Your STORY, And YOUR PURPOSE Awaits You, My Love.

JOURNAL #110

◀◦IMPULSIVE Individuals Are DANGER ZONES

Runnnn From Those Types Of RELATION-ships, FRIEND-ships, & BUSINESS-ships!!!! ◀◦

●IMPULSIVENESS = NO SINCERE HEARING & OR OBEDIENCE FROM GOD.●

There Is NO WAY You're Able To Listen To God If You're An Impulsive Individual. LISTENING Requires WAITING...Waiting To Hear His Voice, Waiting To Hear Your CORRECT Next Move, WAITING To Hear The Right Thing(s) To Speak, The Right Way To Respond, Etc....

IMPULSIVENESS Ultimately Leads To DESTRUCTIVENESS Don't Allow That To Be A Trait You Consume My Loves!!!

JOURNAL #III

Many Times We Feel Stuck Because The Things We're Holding On To Are The Very Things Holding Us Back.....Give Yourself Permission To Let Go!!!!

Oh & ALWAYS Remember No Matter Who You Are, No Matter Where You Are, What You've Done, Or Where You've Been...

LISTEN Yo, You Are Deserving Of LOVE That Doesn't Require You To Suffer First!!!

GET IT? GOT IT? GOOD!!

JOURNAL #112

One of the most amazing things about life is GOD HEALS & He
REVEALS…..Put Your trust in the one who KNOWS ALL, SEE'S ALL
And HAS IT ALL IN CONTROL!

JOURNAL #113

Break through your silence and VOICE it into PURPOSE!

JOURNAL #114

Unbelief of purpose not only belittles the acts of God himself, but it also lacks the FULL Concept of who YOU are & who he's created you to be. NOTHING God creates is made by accident. No matter the magnitude there is a SPECIFIC PURPOSE for one's life.

JOURNAL #115

Saying you don't care about what others think to a CERTAIN degree is ignorance. It's imperative to know the difference between VALIDATION (from others) & GOD-Lead identity/ care for others.

JOURNAL #116

Having flaws & having severe issues (mentally) are two totally different things. Mental health Assurance is imperative, especially in the African American community. However, it is the most overlooked demographic due to "US" (Blacks) Adapting & feeling as if instability, toxicity, brokenness, Confusion, obvious psychological disorder traits are "normal". We're so prone to adversity & dysfunction(s) We overlook the imperative-ness of HEALTH & HEALING And that brings about generational bondage/damage. We MUST do better. Let's hold ourselves accountable to seek the necessary healing & help that not only we deserve BUT Our children and children's children as well.

JOURNAL #117

Most of the time the enemy knows who we are before we have even grasped the belief in who we are ourselves. He knows the version of us that God created before we were even placed into our mother's womb; & that is why he uses every tactic he can think of to demolish that version of us..... BUT Once we become FULLY aware of who God created us to be. We will walk boldly & unapologetically in our Authenticity/Purpose. He tries you because he knows of the version of you that you can't even see he's ultimately AFRAID Of who you will be.

JOURNAL #118

God Can Not Bless Who We Pretend To Be; Or Who We Desire To Be...
He Can Only Bless Who HE CALLED YOU TO BE!!! Walk Boldly &
Unapologetically In Your GOD-Given Purpose...Man Has No Power Over
Your Validation If You're In The Room It's Because He's QUALIFIED
You To Be There. Work Your Lane W/God-fidence Humility & No Regret.

JOURNAL #119

Sis, Yea It Hurts BUT I Need For You To Take Accountability For Allowing Someone To Continuously Hurt You......The Problem Is We As Women Always Desire To Be Captain "SAVE A MAN; HE'S JUST BROKEN...I CAN HELP HIM CHANGE" ....You CAN'T Help ANYONE Change Who Doesn't Want To CHANGE & Get The Necessary & PROPER Help They Need ......You've Lost Yourself At The Expense Of Damaged Goods Himself & NO YOU AREN'T PERFECT EITHER BUT You Gave It Your ALL...CRY, SCREAM, PRAY, PRAY & PRAY Even More.....BUT You MUST Know That ACCOUNTABILITY Is Needed In Every Way.

JOURNAL #120

In times of turmoil, we need Friendships, & Relationships That Will Build Us up as Oppose to Mentally & Verbally Tearing Us Down.

JOURNAL #121

Taking precautions when someone's heart is placed into your hands.

Life is Real, People are real & time is limited....it is imperative that when we encounter people. We take precautions of their heart. Meaning the state it's in now & even the state it was in before you. People don't always share their previous growing pains & when they do they trust you to not invoke that pain back on to them for another round. How are you helping to release the burden off of someone's life w/your everyday acts of love?! ♥.

JOURNAL #122

Hold Yourself Accountable For The Way In Which You Allowed Someone To Treat You BUT Don't Allow Your Accountability To Diminish & Or Overtake The Fact That THEY Still Hurt You. BALANCE Your KNOWLEDGE/Portion of SELF HURT— INFLECTION & YOUR INDICATOR of PAIN!

JOURNAL #123

It doesn't matter what type of dysfunctions and suffering MOST people go through...That IS NOT An indication that you have to accept and or put up with it too. This universe, unfortunately, operates predominately on SURVIVAL & BROKENNESS ❤ ......THAT DOES NOT Place ME In A Position To Be Willing To Just Accept That As Well....NO! LOVE & WHOLENESS Is What Truly Brings About Strength.....See SURVIVAL & BROKENNESS is the COWARD "feel bad for me" way out.....NO, You MUST HEAL! HEAL! HEAL! There Is Absolutely NOTHING Cute & or Attractive about being broken and trying to drag others into brokenness with you.

JOURNAL #124

For every life walked & for every breath taken there's a GOD-Ordained calling and intent for you and your life.

JOURNAL #125

REPEAT AFTER ME:

Life is all about perspective and my perspective is through the lens of Christ.

JOURNAL #126

God can not heal without brokenness of one's self being revealed... be honest with WHAT BROKE you so that WHOLENESS Can CONSUME you. Even if that WHAT, is YOU!

JOURNAL #127

Never comment on someone's life story, trials and or situation(s) because we don't know what goes on behind what is at face value. There is always BOTH sides AND then there's GOD'S TRUTH!!! So simply say a prayer for others & focus on what pertains to YOU!.

ABOUT THE AUTHOR

Racquel Cooney is a 26 year old singer, actress, writer (expressionist), journalism major, purpose influencer, and founder of the Beyond Peculiar Movement. Beyond Peculiar is a movement that encourages individuals to be true to their authentic selves. Whom God has created them to be. Beyond Peculiar is a movement that also ignites purpose and fuels destiny. Cooney believes that we were ALL created to stand out, and that it is our duty to shine our light and allow it to shine effortlessly, unapologetically, and boldly in the most peculiar way possible (1st Peter 2:9). "I live to help awaken the purpose and gifts that unknowingly lives on the inside of others. I believe that there is a divine purpose and destiny for each and every human being God has placed upon this earth. God has created you, gifted you, anointed you, and appointed you to live and manifest the purpose and gifts that are on the inside of you" (Cooney).

Cooney believes that it is imperative to become all that God has created us to be. Even if it unintentionally makes others feel uncomfortable. She encourages others to grow through what they go through so that others can get through. Cooney believes that sharing your story is a two-way street. It unveils the pain in you while setting your brother and or sister free. "Your voice and the very essence of your being is needed my love" (Cooney).

CONNECT WITH RACQUEL

Racquel Cooney's goal is to continuously inspire, encourage, and empower young men and women to be and reach the best version of themselves; who God has created them to be. Racquel is a purpose influencer who presents the knowledge of God-fidence and wholeness at women retreats, non-profit organizations, schools, and church functions. In 2018 she launched the Beyond Peculiar "Awaken Your Purpose" tour. She made it her duty to use her motivational platform by travelling to different schools and recreational centers to help motivate, cultivate, and ignite change for the betterment of our upcoming generation's destiny. It is no secret that due to the instant gratification of our society children, teens, and young adults all across the globe have gained a false ideology as it pertains to PURPOSE and SUCCESS. So many have idolized social media's perception of success, beauty, and leadership. Cooney has made it her responsibility to help awaken the PURPOSE that lives on the inside of each student/teen. If they are unaware of what their purpose is this tour will help navigate them into the right direction.

  Beyond Peculiar cooneyracquel@ymail.com

Printed in the United States
By Bookmasters